VICTORIOUS LIVING

VICTORIOUS LIVING

7 KEYS TO A VICTORIOUS LIFE

DR. C.L. SPELLS, SR.

PUBLISHED BY
HARVEST LAND MINISTRIES, INC.

Copyright © 2012 by Dr. C.L. Spells, Sr.

ISBN 978-0-615-51279-2

All rights reserved. No portion of this book may be reproduced in any form, stored in a retrieval system, or transmitted in any form by any means – electronic, mechanical, photocopy, recording scanning or otherwise – except for brief quotations in critical reviews or articles, without the written permission of Dr. C.L. Spells, Sr.

Published in Hampton, VA by Harvest Land Ministries, Inc.

Cover and interior layout and design by David "3D" Ferreira of MASTERGRAFIX.com.

Editing by Robin Page of Kingdom Living Day by Day, LLC.

Unless otherwise indicated, Scripture quotations in this book are taken from the Holy Bible, King James Version.

Scripture quotations marked (NIV) are taken from the HOLY BIBLE, NEW INTERNATIONAL VERSION®. NIV®. Copyright© 1973, 1978, 1984 by International Bible Society. Used by permission of Zondervan. All rights reserved.

Scripture quotations taken from the New American Standard Bible®, Copyright © 1960, 1962, 1963, 1968, 1971, 1972, 1973, 1975, 1977, 1995 by The Lockman Foundation
Used by permission. (www.Lockman.org)

Verses marked NKJV are taken from the New King James Version. Copyright © 1979, 1980, 1982 by Thomas Nelson, Inc. Used by permission. All rights reserved.

Second Edition - 2012

Acknowledgments

All honor and glory belongs to our God.

I would like to take this time to say thank you to my wife, Pastor Christina Spells. You are to me everything that I could ever ask God for. Your love, affection, anointing, and prophetic gifting has been an immeasurable force in my life. I love you!

To my children Destiny, Chris Jr., and Caleb. I love you all so much. I'm truly blessed to be your father. Even greater things than these shall God do through you.

A special thanks to Apostle Steven W. Banks and Dr. Keira Banks. What a mantle, Thank you for your love, support, and your covering.

I would like to thank my father, Deacon MacArthur Spells and my mother, Fannie Spells. Your constant prayers have been my blessing.

Special thanks to the Harvest Land Ministries International family. Your dedication, faithfulness, and continual support have been remarkable. Double portion of blessings to you all.

TABLE OF CONTENTS

FOREWORD	IX
INTRODUCTION	XI
CHAPTER I – SALVATION: THE KEY TO VICTORY	1
CHAPTER II – THE COVENANT	9
CHAPTER III – THE WAYS OF THE FATHER	15
CHAPTER IV – HAPPINESS VS. JOY	25
CHAPTER V – DESIGNED BY GOD	39
CHAPTER VI – DAVID'S ANOINTING	75
CHAPTER VII – KINGDOM ASSIGNMENT	85
NOTES	93
ABOUT THE AUTHOR	95

Foreword

Dr. C.L Spells has delivered a treasure for anyone who desires to move out of the complacent and mediocre, and into a lifestyle of Victorious Living. This calls for commitment, dedication and discipline. In his book, Victorious Living, Dr. Spells explores the notion that most people fail to live this kind of life because of an inability to see how and what God sees, as well as the reality of the busy, fast-paced world that we live in. He skillfully shares with the reader a plethora of ways in which we can exercise our "God-given" abilities within us and come out of every situation as overcomers.

Dr. Spells shares insight on how to stay connected to the source of all victory. He lays out a Biblical foundation that is sure to have you on your way to living that life of Victory that God has promised to you. As you apply the tools within this book, you will begin to see in ways that you have never seen before, and it will cause you to shift your mindset from average to triumphant; from mediocre to successful; from defeat to Victory!

Dr. Spells himself is a victorious husband and father, victorious pastor, victorious businessman. This is a practical application from a spiritual son whose commitment and assignment is to produce an overcoming kingdom-minded people.

Enjoy!

Steven W. Banks,
Chief Apostle & Presiding Bishop
Living Waters International Alliance
Newport News, Virginia

Introduction

Being aligned with God's will for your life is essential to living in Kingdom prosperity. Let's face it. Many Christians live a life filled with 28 hours of work to be accomplished in a 24-hour time span. From the time we get up in the morning and have devotions, get dressed, eat a quick breakfast and dash out the door, to homework with the kids, bathing, cooking, cleaning, eating dinner, and having family time, life can seem to be more laborious than joyful. Stress and dissatisfaction with life has become the common theme. It seems as if our lives have become a stage play in which we are merely a character who subsequently has a very small role. This feeling can be overwhelming to say the least. But the chaos stops here! God has allowed you to have this book in your hands so that you can become realigned with your Kingdom destiny. First things first. You are not crazy and you are not alone. We all find ourselves in a place of frustration in different seasons of our lives, but God has created us to be overcomers.

| VICTORIOUS LIVING

The Bible says in John 10:10, "The thief cometh not, but for to steal, and to kill, and to destroy: I am come that they might have life, and that they might have it more abundantly." Notice that He said, "life, and that they might have it more abundantly." A more abundant life is your Kingdom inheritance and by the grace of God I pray that after you read this book you experience nothing less.

Chapter I

SALVATION: THE KEY TO VICTORY

Salvation

> *"For whatsoever is born of God overcometh the world: and this is the victory that overcometh the world, even our faith"*
>
> 1 John 5:4

Accepting Jesus Christ as Lord and Savior of your life is the gateway to true prosperity. When you become born again you are deputized with power from on high to overcome every obstacle, crisis, and challenge that you face. So often I hear people say that they know Jesus or that they have a personal relationship with God. However, a relationship is not merely running

| VICTORIOUS LIVING

to someone in a time of need. Many think that just because they consider themselves to be good people that they are in good standing with God and that they are covered by God's favor, are blessed, and are worthy to spend eternity in Heaven. But No! It does not work that way. The truth is that there are going to be a lot of good people who unfortunately may find themselves in Hell. Now I know that in this current era when someone brings up the "H" word it clears the room, but God is a God of truth. We cannot take the liberty to alter His rules for fear of offending others, not being well liked, or simply just going along to get along. Believers have a responsibility to encourage others in the Word of God. Not doing so assists the enemy in his plight against mankind and hinders others in their quest to be free from the bondage of this world. Here is an example for consideration: Two good people met in college and began a relationship. After college they both landed great jobs and purchased a home together. They are both very courteous, kind to others, liked among their peers, and heavily involved in positive deeds in their community. Wow! With this resume it sounds as if they are guaranteed a pass into Heaven's

SALVATION: THE KEY TO VICTORY | I

gates. They certainly seem good enough, but this good without receiving the salvation of Jesus Christ is simply just one too many o's. Everything that we do must be of God.

> *"For by grace are ye saved through faith; and that not of yourselves: it is the gift of God: Not of works, lest any man should boast"*
>
> *Eph. 2:8*

Salvation is a gift from God, and the work aspect of our redemption was done and accomplished over two thousand years ago. All that we have to do now is follow the pattern set for us in the Book of Romans. Romans 10:9 says, "That if thou shalt confess with thy mouth the Lord Jesus, and shalt believe in thine heart that God hath raised him from the dead, thou shalt be saved". Now, it is not my practice to condemn anyone or to restrict anyone from establishing a relationship with Christ no matter what his or her struggles may be. However, we must keep in mind that a Kingdom lifestyle yields kingdom results. Yes, these two people can live together, accomplish wonderful feats and

| VICTORIOUS LIVING

live the American dream, but they will not receive a heavenly reward unless they operate according to the Word of God. Without God there is no covenant; therefore, there is no fulfillment of God's promises and divine plans for your life. So often when I leave my home on Sundays to go to church I see these kinds of couples. They are mowing the lawn on a sunny Sunday morning or sitting on their decks enjoying life as their outdoor speakers softly release the sound of smooth jazz in preparation for an evening grill. Now, having fun and enjoying life is the will of God. It is really the heart of God that Christians would do so more often, but not while forfeiting our Kingdom responsibilities and the duties that go along with being in covenant. Being in covenant with God is key because no matter what takes place in your life, you are covered by God's grace. The Word of God declares in Psalm 37:25 "I have been young, and now am old; yet have I not seen the righteous forsaken, nor his seed begging bread". Seeing successful people who are not convicted about their lack of covenant with God can be quite deceptive and perceived as victorious living but it is not the case. Anyone that works hard and is disciplined can acquire money, homes and material things, but victorious living is not just about acquiring something, it is having the peace, provision, wisdom, protection, and favor of God in every arena of your life.

Relationships

I watched a television show the other day as a young lady competed for a job. The show always asks the contestants at the end of their task who they thought the weakest team members were and the two contestants with the most votes are asked to come before the judges and plead their case as to why they should not be fired. One young lady who was very well spoken and educated seemed to be unliked by her peers and it looked as if she was going to be sent home. But as fate would have it, the judges voted the other contestant off and not her. Well, after she won she went back to the green room ranting, raving, and cursing into the camera about how unstoppable she was and then without hesitation or reservation she proceeded to say how blessed she was and how God's favor was upon her. Victorious living is not placing an artificial stamp of approval of God on things that we have done,

| VICTORIOUS LIVING

acquired or conjured up in our carnal minds without consulting Him first.

> *"Not every one that saith unto me, Lord, Lord, shall enter into the kingdom of heaven; but he that doeth the will of my Father which is in heaven. Many will say to me in that day, Lord, Lord, have we not prophesied in thy name? and in thy name have cast out devils? and in thy name done many wonderful works? And then will I profess unto them, I never knew you: depart from me, ye that work iniquity. Therefore whosoever heareth these sayings of mine, and doeth them, I will liken him unto a wise man, which built his house upon a rock: And the rain descended, and the floods came, and the winds blew, and beat upon that house; and it fell not: for it was founded upon a rock. And every one that heareth these sayings of mine, and doeth them not, shall be likened unto a foolish man, which built his house upon the sand: And the*

SALVATION: THE KEY TO VICTORY | 1

> *rain descended, and the floods came, and the winds blew, and beat upon that house; and it fell: and great was the fall of it"*
>
> *Matt. 7: 21–27*

See, both men were able to build the house. The difference is that one house fell and the other house stood. Why? Because it was not the elements of the storm that determined the fate of each house but rather what the houses were built upon. Victorious living is building every aspect of your life on the word of God. This fact is why Psalm 127: 1 says, "EXCEPT the LORD build the house, they labour in vain that build it: except the LORD keep the city, the watchman waketh but in vain." Without the salvation of God there is no victory- only an illusion. Victorious living is not avoiding crisis because they are unavoidable. Victorious living is about building your life upon the rock of Jesus Christ who gives you the power to withstand any storm and to declare to recession, divorce, foreclosure, bankruptcy, afflictions, etc. that you are an overcomer.

| **VICTORIOUS** LIVING

THE COVENANT

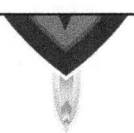

Living for Jesus Christ is not for the faint at heart. This is why so many people do their best to avoid those who attempt to share the Word of God with them. I call those who are willing to share "Kingdom recruiters". They recruit non-believers to become converted into believers and it is not an easy job. When asked about enlisting in the army of the Lord most people try to create what I like to call "reserve duty". Reserve duty means that they do not want to serve unless it is at a convenient time. When 9-11 occurred many enlisted soldiers requested to separate from the military. When asked why, off the record, many stated that they joined to go to college. Others stated things such as family

VICTORIOUS LIVING

needs, medical benefits, etc. But soldiers must have the integrity to walk out the call. It cannot just be about the benefits of military life. When you become a part of any institution that you are involved in and you do not value the corporate goal of the unit you will find that in times of hardship the thought of severing ties will be at the forefront of your mind. Victorious living however, is not just what is beneficial to you but what is pleasing unto God. When you are in covenant with God you must understand that what pleases God will in turn bless you.

> *"Blessed be the Lord, who daily loadeth us with benefits"*   Psa. 68:19

When you become a true son of God you know He takes care of His children. The reason that most people cannot serve God correctly is because they do so from the perspective of a servant. Their eyes are so fixated on their prosperity they forget that there is only one way to truly prosper.

THE COVENANT

"If ye then, being evil, know how to give good gifts unto your children, how much more shall your Father which is in heaven give good things to them that ask him?"

Matt 7:11

We must have faith to believe God in order to receive what He has promised.

To believe is to know Him as Father and not just your source for increase. In the house of God you have many levels: babe, childish children, servant and son. These speak to levels of relationship.

1. ***Babes*** - are by nature selfish because of their immaturity. They normally can do very little for themselves. They must be taught and then weaned from dependency.

2. ***Childish children*** - have grown in time yet not in spirit. They often still need special attention when they should be leading others themselves.

| VICTORIOUS LIVING

3. *Servants* - are those who operate in a strong sense of carnality. When they give they expect an immediate return. They serve with a false sense of entitlement, without the revelation of an heir's inheritance.

4. *Sons* - those who are born into the Kingdom through salvation. Their heart is to please the Father at all times.

WHEN YOU ARE IN COVENANT WITH GOD YOU MUST UNDERSTAND THAT WHAT PLEASES GOD WILL IN TURN BLESS YOU.

Galatians 4:1 says, "Now I say, That the heir, as long as he is a child, differeth nothing from a servant, though he be lord of all". This means that all of Heaven is at our access but it cannot be released to us until we mature into a son of God. A son knows God as Father and a servant only knows Him as master. As a child I was raised on a farm and it was a lot of hard work. After school, when most kids were able to come home and watch television and do their homework, I came in, got a snack and went right out to feed the animals and attend to the farm. I was not the least enthused about this chapter of my life and did not desire to do my chores. Yet I remember expressing my disdain about the farm life when my father asked me to go into the field with him. He began to explain that he needed my help but was hurt to see my lack of desire to assist him, and with a calm voice and tears in his eyes he told me, "Son, you don't have to come". When I looked in his eyes I saw his hurt and his pain. Of course after seeing his pain I went with him. While in the field I apologized for my immature actions. My dad later expressed that he did not understand why I did not want to help him help me. He explained that his harvest from the farm helped send my sister to college and to buy my school clothes. I think back on that encounter now and say to myself that must be how God feels about mankind.

> *"And grieve not the Holy Spirit of God, whereby ye are sealed unto the day of redemption"*   Eph. 4:30

Now, God asks us to do things that seem laborious and inconvenient to us due to our selfish ambitions, but in the end they are working for our good. On that day I graduated from a servant to that of a son. A true son never wants to see his father grieve.

CHAPTER III
THE WAYS OF THE FATHER

> *"Jesus saith unto him, I am the way, the truth, and the life: no man cometh unto the Father, but by me"*   John 14:6

We preach "come as you are" but Christ never intended for you to stay as you are. The more you learn about Him, the greater your opportunity to change yourself into His likeness and His image.

> *"He made known his ways unto Moses, his acts unto the children of Israel"*   Psa. 103:7

Many of you know the acts of God through His forgiveness, love, provision, and more. All of these are

| VICTORIOUS LIVING

actions that show the hand of the Lord blessing you. However there are times that God shapes your life through the encounters with the Pharaohs, Goliaths and Herods of the world that cause you to ask God: "Why does it seem as if the world is against me? Did I do something wrong?" But notice the scripture said that He made known both His acts and His ways, meaning that if you know something then you should be acting like you know it. Jesus Christ is the only way to find victory in the midst of adversity. He is the way. We have to look at what He did to fulfill His call in order to fulfill ours.

> *"WHEREFORE, holy brethren, partakers of the heavenly calling, consider the Apostle and High Priest of our profession, Christ Jesus"*
>
> *Heb 3:1*

The heavenly calling is the calling of salvation or the giving of your life as a sacrifice. This is what Jesus did on Calvary and what we do everyday as we seek after Him. Matthew 16:24 says, "Then said Jesus unto his disciples, If any man will come after me, let him

THE WAYS OF THE FATHER | III

deny himself, and take up his cross, and follow me." The cross is a place of suffering and with no cross there will be no crown. The scripture said, "if any man comes after me." This means that if someone desires to operate in Jesus' power and anointing that he must defeat the world by operating in the unseen promises of God - even when the pain and anguish of the world mounts up against him. You must have a mind to complete your call. Having the father's heart gives the son a spirit of a finisher.

> *"When Jesus therefore had received the vinegar, he said, "It is finished: "and he bowed his head, and gave up the ghost"*
>
> *John 19:30*

Jesus completed the will of His Father. In Luke 9:62 "Jesus said unto him, No man, having put his hand to the plough, and looking back, is fit for the kingdom of God". You must have a made up mind and say to yourself everyday, "I'm not going to give up because God is in control". There is a sense of peace even in the midst of warfare when you know the ways of God.

| VICTORIOUS LIVING

According to 2 Timothy 1:12 "If we suffer, we shall also reign with him". God is your Father and He would never let the enemy get away with harming you. The enemy thinks that he can make things so hard for you that you will forfeit your Kingdom identity to seek comfort, revenge, or riches. Nevertheless, you have victory over the wiles of the enemy and you have the revelation that God is not unaware of any of your hardship. Hebrews 10:30 says, "I will recompense, saith the Lord. And again, The Lord shall judge his people." This means that we can rejoice knowing that God has taken account of everything that we have lost and will recompense us in every way.

WE PREACH "COME AS YOU ARE" BUT CHRIST NEVER INTENDED FOR YOU TO STAY AS YOU ARE.

DEVELOP YOUR CHARACTER

Living an "active duty" life as someone who continuously represents the Kingdom of God is what you need to strive to do. Let's face it, no one is perfect. The saving grace is that you have a perfect God. In spite of any of your imperfections you must never attempt

THE WAYS OF THE FATHER | III

to restructure the Word of God to accommodate your lifestyle. At times things can get hard and very tempting. But do not compromise with your carnal mind. Now, no one has been able to enter the earth and leave without any sin besides Jesus Christ. I say that because as you pursue the Kingdom lifestyle I do not want you to become frustrated and think that it is unattainable. However, I do want you to know that it is a process by which you learn how to live better daily. The Bible tells you in 2 Corinthians 3:6 "not of the letter, but of the spirit: for the letter killeth, but the spirit giveth life".

You deserve the very best and you do not have to settle for less than what your Heavenly Father has promised you. My father always used to tell me; "Son, if you're going to do something do it right or don't do it at all." He did not say this with expectation that I would do everything perfect but even in my shortcomings he inspired me to do it to the best of my ability. There are many things that you can do to better your quality of life. However, no matter what you do it does not exempt you from tests, trials and seasons of change.

| VICTORIOUS LIVING

So often you may become frustrated with life's challenges. Quite naturally this causes you to begin to strategize. You look for ways to find that place of happiness that you often like to recall and talk about from the past. Reminiscing is something that everyone does; however, the reality is that even if you were to revisit some of the same things that you used to do they still would not bring you the same satisfaction. Nor will it bring to you the same fulfillment that you were accustomed to in your past. This is because over the years of your life you have matured and therefore, changed. The only constant in your life without Jesus Christ is the element of change. Certainly life is full of inconsistencies, but when you accept Jesus Christ into your life He becomes the constant or "model". He equips you to be able to stand and continue to experience the peace that surpasses all of your understanding while encountering the different seasons that life brings. Even in times of uncertainty, when you seem lost and you do not know which way to go, God is the constant reminder of the hope of your calling. The heart of Jesus Christ is to teach you who you are and how valuable and important you are to

THE WAYS OF THE FATHER | III

your Heavenly Father. His will is to see you operate in excellence as men and women of destiny and vision.

> *"Every good gift and every perfect gift is from above, and cometh down from the Father of lights, with whom is no variableness, neither shadow of turning"*   Jam. 1:17

There is no variableness in God and if you want to consistently improve your quality of life and are determined to live victoriously there must be a constant place of focus in your inner man that does not waver during times of crisis. This kind of discipline can only be made possible by cultivating a Kingdom mindset. The Bible tells us, "but let him ask in faith, nothing wavering. For he that wavereth is like a wave of the sea driven with the wind and tossed. For let not that man think that he shall receive any thing of the Lord. A double minded man is unstable in all his ways" (James 1:6-8).

| VICTORIOUS LIVING

Disappointment is the child of false expectations. Placing your faith in God's Word is truly the answer to every question that life brings. Your problems in life can usually be linked to your lack of understanding.

WE HAVE TO LOOK AT WHAT HE DID TO FULFILL HIS CALL IN ORDER TO FULFILL OURS.

Problems work against those who are unaware of how to solve them and this is why Hosea 4:6 says, "My people are destroyed for lack of knowledge". When you place your faith in God and get a revelation of what you need to adjust in your life to continue to prosper, you alter your current situation and change from one who has a problem to one who is noted to be a problem solver. As you meditate on the Word of God you must do so knowing that He is as sovereign as His Word. There are two things that never change about God and these two things are His promise and His performance. Believing that God's Word is going to come to pass is the prerequisite for its manifestation. As a child my parents often reminded me of what they expected of me when we went in certain venues, whether it was a store, church or visiting someone's home. Their expectation was directly connected to my behavior. I knew that if I behaved there was going to be a blessing on the other side of my ability to display the discipline that they instilled in me as their child. Even as a child you learn how to discipline your behavior in spite of your desires. Why, sure, it would have been more interesting to roam around the store on my own, to talk to my friends in church, or to touch one of the many ornaments that my aunt had on her living room table when we went to visit, but my faith in the reward outweighed my natural inclinations to waver. Is it possible that at times your faith misbehaves? Well, God says that when it does misbehave do not think that you are going to find victory at the end of your endeavors. God's will is that you understand His expectations and develop a faith based behavior pattern that causes you not to waver while pursuing His will for your life.

Salvation, as it relates to your destiny, is the God given power to become what God has eternally decreed you were before the foundation of the world. What people so often refer to as grace truly is God's divine

| VICTORIOUS LIVING

enablement to accomplish your predestined purpose. When the Lord says to Paul in 2 Corinthians 12:9 "My grace is sufficient for thee: for my strength is made perfect in weakness," He is simply stating that His power is not limited to our circumstances. You are empowered by God to reach and accomplish goals that transcend human limitations!

CHAPTER IV

HAPPINESS VS. JOY

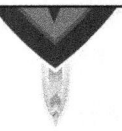

Many people fell in love with the movie *The Pursuit Of Happyness*. While I thought the movie was OK, I thought the title could be perceived incorrectly. See, happiness is a state of well being characterized by emotions. However emotions are not feelings that are contrived from the outside but rather they are developed internally. Whether you like it or not, everyone has emotions. The goal is to not be ruled by your emotions. The Bible says in Hebrews 10:38, "now the just shall live by faith" however most people live by their emotions or feelings. Ironically this is how Satan causes you to devalue yourself. He deceives you with the thoughts, feelings, and concepts that influence mankind to go after the cares of this world. While chasing happiness most Christians find themselves subjugating their God

| VICTORIOUS LIVING

> ### THE KEY IS NOT TO PURSUE HAPPINESS BUT TO PURSUE JESUS.

given blessings to a dollar amount or material things to invoke feelings of success. The harsh reality is that feelings are degenerative and material things that you acquire are as well. When was the last time you wore a suit that you purchased ten years ago? Can you imagine how much a dealership would give someone for a car that they purchased brand new just one year prior? Well I did the research and "PF Investing" says that the depreciation in the first year itself is an astonishing 18-28%. Not that you should be wearing old clothes or driving around in a hoopty, but know that you cannot scratch a spiritual itch with a physical fix. This is why I pondered the movie's title because emotions are depreciative, degenerative and subject to change as well. You can be happy one day and sad the next. Just suppose the man in the movie did not get the job that he applied for? Does that mean he should give up hope? Does that give him the right to go into a season of depression? Do riches necessarily equate to happiness? I do recall in the movie the man losing his wife and he seemed to really love her. I wonder what the price tag is on true love. I personally know many unhappy people who are subsequently very rich. The danger of pursuing happiness is that happiness is based upon what is happening and dictated by the happenstances of life. What if your life is not making you happy today? The key is not to pursue happiness but to pursue Jesus. Many people find happiness in what they do for the moment yet they find themselves unhappy with the final results. The adulterer does not like the cost of divorce. The alcoholic does not like the hangover. The smoker does not like cancer. The overeater does not like obesity.

In order to walk in victory in the midst of warfare you must pattern yourself after Jesus. Take a look and observe how He overcame such adversity.

> *"Looking unto Jesus the author and finisher of our faith; who for the joy that was set before him endured the cross, despising the shame, and is set down at the right hand of the throne of God"*   Heb. 12:2

| VICTORIOUS LIVING

Notice that the text says for the "joy" that was set before Him. Happiness is a degenerative emotion but joy is a realm of strength. Nehemiah 8:10 says, "Then he said unto them, Go your way, eat the fat, and drink the sweet, and send portions unto them for whom nothing is prepared: for this day is holy unto our Lord: neither be ye sorry; for the 'joy of the LORD is your strength'". To the believer, joy is the spiritual disposition that enables them to have faith and confidence in God, no matter what their circumstances are. If you have purchased or inherited an item that is of extreme value, it is wise to take out an insurance policy on the item knowing that it is of extreme value and cannot be easily replaced. When believers set their faith dial on joy just as Jesus did they can endure the cross and despise the shame while going through different seasons of life. They know that God sees His children as His most prized possession and as an All Wise God He has not taken out an insurance policy but rather He has placed His blessed assurance on your lives. This truth is why most of God's people do not suffer from anxiety when there is a lack of apparent victory and when it seems as if things are not happening in their

HAPPINESS VS. JOY | IV

favor. They are fully aware that there are mysteries at work in the unseen realm. While people often try to figure things out, God takes time to work things out for those who obey Him and align their faith and their works together. Isn't it wonderful to know that even as you go through your trials there are blessings being developed in the unseen realm that God shall cause to manifest because of your faithfulness? When you have the revelation of God's thoughts and plans towards you, you are fully persuaded that your life will continually prosper. In Jeremiah 29:11 it states, "For I know the thoughts that I think toward you, saith the LORD, thoughts of peace, and not of evil, to give you an expected end." Many people encounter the trials and hardships of one season and approach them as if their world is coming to an end. But no, it is not the end.

WORKING CONSTANTLY WITHOUT TIME OF MEDITATION AND PRAYER WILL NEVER ALLOW YOU TO CLEAR YOUR HEAD OF YOUR DAY-TO-DAY DUTIES.

For every bad day there is a better day. For every sad day there is a brighter day. No matter how you cut the pie, if you exercise your faith and take on

VICTORIOUS LIVING

a Kingdom mindset you will get a slice of victory every time. The key however is to seek the voice of the Lord on a daily basis to receive the revelation that God has for you pertaining to your purpose and Kingdom assignment in the earth. In order to receive the instruction concerning your future you must take time out and spend time with the Lord. Working constantly without time of meditation and prayer will never allow you to clear your head of your day-to-day duties. Sometimes life itself can become a bundle of confusion even when you are doing positive things. There must be an inward peace that comes only from the Word of God. Without this peace in your heart, you would literally fail in the days of adversity. You are living in a nation that has declared that you are in a failing economy. The reality is that if you have the revelation of the Kingdom of God you have the power to overcome the powers and the bondage of this world. But the inward peace that gives you this power only comes when you cultivate the presence of the Lord into your life on a regular basis. This act allows Him to release His directions and plans as it pertains to where you should go and what it is that you need to do to continue to prosper. Without inner peace, no matter what you accomplish in life, you will always question whether or not you are living in your ordained calling. There is nothing more frustrating than to wonder if you are maximizing your life or settling for less. However, when you are pursuing Christ daily you may not know all of the details but you do know that you are in the hands of the One who does. When you understand this revelation you cease to worry about the unknown or unforeseen.

> *"And the peace of God, which passeth all understanding, shall keep your hearts and minds through Christ Jesus"*   Phil. 4:7

You need to know that even though things may seem insurmountable, you are going to make it. The Bible says, "while the earth remaineth, seedtime and harvest, and cold and heat, and summer and winter, and day and night shall not cease" (Gen. 8:22). Just as the earth cycles through the seasons of the year and just as they are all equally important and serve their own God ordained purpose, you cycle through seasons of your life that are important to your ordained purpose. They all serve a purpose that you may not see at that very moment. However, the good news is that the strength of the storm does not measure up to the beauty of God's restoration. Do not dare give up!

Quitting is not an option. Most people quit when they are so close to their breakthrough. Whenever you have breakthrough in the spirit realm Satan gets nervous because he knows that he is losing his grip concerning the afflictions and hardship that occur in your life. However, in times of intense warfare you learn both who you are and who God is. I know that times of hardship can be draining spiritually, mentally and physically. Exhaustion can easily cause you to spend your time looking for a way out rather than a way to find victory. You must apply yourself in order to maximize every season that you encounter. Yes there are times in your day-to-day walk with Christ that you do need times of consecration; however you are not always afforded this luxury. When Satan launches warfare into your environment he does not play by the rules. You have to overcome his attacks. You cannot leave your assignment half done. You must be aware that Satan always makes his last hurrah on his way out. His mantra is "if I can't rule the entire house, the least that I can do is set a few rooms on fire on my way out". But what happens when you are frustrated about the way things are going? What do you do after you pay the unforeseen bill or go through an ordeal that was totally uncomfortable? Many make the vital mistake of declaring a negative future. They place limitations on their future capabilities by saying negative confessions. For example; "if something else happens wrong I'm going to lose my mind, I just won't be able to take it."

EXHAUSTION CAN EASILY CAUSE YOU TO SPEND YOUR TIME LOOKING FOR A WAY OUT RATHER THAN A WAY TO FIND VICTORY.

Many often take it as a sign that the fight is over and that is when the enemy launches an even greater attack because he wants to break you down. But you must remember Philippians 1:6 says, "being confident of this very thing, that he which hath begun a good work in you will perform it until the day of Jesus Christ". It is important to know that even when you are at your wits

| VICTORIOUS LIVING

end that God is still fighting on your behalf. God just wants you to keep the faith. In Moses' time of warfare, God told Moses, who then told the people, "Fear ye not, stand still, and see the salvation of the LORD, which he will shew to you today: for the Egyptians whom ye have seen today, ye shall see them again no more for ever. The LORD shall fight for you, and ye shall hold your peace" (Exo. 14:13 – 14). Notice that the scripture says fear not. What you fear you serve. This is why it states in Proverbs 9:10 "the fear of the LORD is the beginning of wisdom: and the knowledge of the holy is understanding". The fear of the Lord is that He is real and that the consequences of sin are detrimental to our salvation as well as our prosperity.

Fearing the enemy is not an option. Even when times seem unbearable this is not the time to throw a pity party. No my friend, wrong soirée. It is time to have a Holy Ghost party! The key to receiving your promise is locked up in your praise. People, who are not skilled or developed in warfare, clam up, shut up, and give up when obstacles arise. When you feel as if you can do

HAPPINESS VS. JOY | IV

no more there is a revelation. In 2 Chronicles 20:15 the Spirit of the Lord states, "hearken ye, all Judah, and ye inhabitants of Jerusalem, and thou king Jehoshaphat, Thus saith the LORD unto you, Be not afraid nor dismayed by reason of this great multitude; for the battle is not yours, but God's". We must remember that according to Ephesians 6:12 we wrestle not against flesh and blood but against principalities and demonic powers that cannot be defeated without God. Our fight according to 1 Timothy 6:12 is to "fight the good fight of faith" but not to entangle ourselves by warring in the natural. If you stay out of the ring and let God fight for you, victory shall be yours. If you do not have this revelation, you may over reach and force things to happen rather than wait on the Lord's intervention.

The Bible tells us in 1 Peter 4:12-13 "Beloved, think it not strange concerning the fiery trial which is to try you, as though some strange thing happened unto you: But rejoice, inasmuch as ye are partakers of Christ's sufferings; that, when his glory shall be revealed, ye may be glad also with exceeding joy."

| VICTORIOUS LIVING

Your attitude towards obstacles will determine your effectiveness in overcoming them. Some consider it faking when you have a positive attitude while enduring a negative situation. However to someone with a Kingdom mindset it is just another opportunity for increase. However, you cannot see it this way unless you have a revelation. A revelation is the revealing or disclosing, through active or passive communication with a supernatural or a divine entity (Wikipedia). Revelation is knowing the heart of the Father concerning any matter. As you seek God and pursue His will for your life He discloses hidden mysteries and shows you the end of a matter before it even starts. This is shown in Romans 8:28, "And we know that all things work together for good to them that love God, to them who are the called according to his purpose." You must learn how God operates. You have to pray and hear the voice of God in your spirit to see just what it is that He is trying to get out of allowing you to grow through carnal altercations in life. I have found that for every trial there is a transaction and when you are going through something normally it has three purposes:

HAPPINESS VS. JOY | IV

1) To purge you of your iniquities.

2) To teach how to operate in the spirit realm in a greater dimension.

3) To establish a testimony so that others can witness the power of God and be converted.

No wonder God tells us to rejoice because this is His process for promotion. This is the revelation that the enemy did not want you to hear. Therefore, when you experience hardships and difficult seasons in your life you become aware that it is a part of God's plan to establish you as an overcomer. You cannot have victory without defeating someone or something.

We know that Christ defeated Satan over two thousand years ago, however there is still a war going on. In 1 Timothy 6:12 it states, "fight the good fight of faith, lay hold on eternal life, whereunto thou art also called, and hast professed a good profession before many witnesses". Beloved we still have to fight! To fight in the mind is to ensure us of the victory awarded to us by our Heavenly Father. This is why, when you hear someone declare that they are living a life of victory, it does not mean that they are living a life without pain, problems, pressure or perplexities; no, that is the next life! Lol! Victorious living simply means as a child of the Most High God according to Isaiah 54:17 "no weapon that is formed against thee shall prosper; and every tongue that shall rise against thee in judgment thou shalt condemn. This is the heritage of the servants of the LORD, and their righteousness is of me, saith the LORD". Notice that it never says that the weapon would not be formed, but it does declare that it shall not prosper or accomplish what it was set out to do. As you read this book open up your mind to the heritage that God has for the body of Christ and by faith receive victory in every arena of your life.

DESIGNED BY GOD

When you look at your life, are you certain of your purpose? Most people spend a great deal of their time accessing what they want to be rather than pursuing what God has called them to be. Jeremiah 1:5 says, "before I formed thee in the belly I knew thee; and before thou camest forth out of the womb I sanctified thee, and I ordained thee a prophet unto the nations". It is a trick of the enemy to cause you to have second thoughts concerning who you are in God. In order to clearly understand the victory available to you, you must first look to the source of your Kingdom identity. Even as children, many try to fit in with others who seem to have life all figured out, gazing at all of the visible trappings that would cause them to desire a life of similar achievements. Many of you pattern

VICTORIOUS LIVING

your life around such individuals forgetting that it is subsequently not what is on the outside that determines the value of how blessed an individual is, but rather what is on the inside. What you see on the outside is often not a true indication of the level of victory on the inside. How often do you see the "Hollywood couple" stroll down the red carpet looking picture perfect only to see them a few months later walking down a dark road of divorce? You must always remember the following passage: "For what shall it profit a man, if he shall gain the whole world, and lose his own soul?" (Mark 8:36). You have authority over everything in the earth as children of God. When you are "born again" you are born from above and you operate from another dimension and view things with a Kingdom perspective. One of today's biggest epidemics is stolen identity. However, even more prevalent is that of mistaken identity.

Someone with a mistaken identity does not know his or her purpose. They can only imitate what they see in the earth because they have not synchronized their soul and spirit with the will of God for their life. Let's take a look at God's purpose for man's creation.

> *"So God created man in his own image, in the image of God created he him; male and female created he them. And God blessed them, and God said unto them, Be fruitful, and multiply, and replenish the earth, and subdue it: and have dominion over the fish of the sea, and over the fowl of the air, and over every living thing that moveth upon the earth"*
>
> Gen. 1:27-28

God created mankind in His image and He blessed them. This blessing is the ability to be co-creators. Here is a list of the characteristics of one who operates according to God's design.

MOST PEOPLE LIVE LIFE FRUSTRATED BY WHAT THEY DO NOT HAVE, BUT GOD HAS DESIGNED US WITH A KINGDOM ASSIGNMENT AND INHERITANCE WITHIN.

| VICTORIOUS LIVING

They have the power to:
1) *Be fruitful*
2) *Multiply*
3) *Replenish*
4) *Subdue*
5) *Have Dominion*

As a co-creator you never seek the things of the earth but rather you are called to be inventors, developers, and builders chosen to impart God's will into the earth. John 14:12 states, "Verily, verily, I say unto you, He that believeth on me, the works that I do shall he do also; and greater works than these shall he do; because I go unto my Father". Most people live life frustrated by what they do not have, but God has designed us with a Kingdom assignment and inheritance within. You already have it. You do not have to seek it. All you have to do is stay the course and it will be made manifest in your life. The limitations or borders of your life do not come from the outside, but rather is an inside job. The scripture says to believe on Him. To believe is an inner peace that takes authority over doubt, fear and anxiety. Doubt, fear and anxiety are all inner borders that come to confine you so you cannot operate according to the will of God for your life. God does the hard work, all you have to do is believe and not become overly anxious to do a thing before it is your season. The Bible says in Revelations 1:8 "I am Alpha and Omega, the beginning and the ending, saith the Lord, which is, and which was, and which is to come, the Almighty." The life that you are living has already been written by God. That is why the book of Hebrews denotes Jesus Christ as an author and a finisher. He knows the script that has been written for you to follow, but you cannot take the liberty to rearrange what He has done to insure your victory. You have been designed to win. How is this so, you may ask? Well, it is because you are designed to be saved.

When you are not saved you live a life that pays horribly. Let's look at the pay scale of a sinner. The Bible states in Romans "for the wages of sin is death". Woe! What a benefits package! If you have not made the decision by now, this would be a great opportunity to empty your desk and let Satan know you quit and that you found more than just new employment but

| VICTORIOUS LIVING

WHEN YOU RECEIVE SALVATION
YOU ARE OFFICIALLY VICTORIOUS.
---

a new life in Jesus Christ because "the gift of God is eternal life through Jesus Christ our Lord" (Rom. 6:23). This is where the saints of God declare victory! When the scripture says "eternal life" it serves notice to every negative season that you are always going to outlive every attack and live in victory. In fact, you are designed to be a victor and not a victim. In 1 John 5:4 it states, "for whatsoever is born of God overcometh the world: and this is the victory that overcometh the world, even our faith". To be saved is to be born again and born of God. To be born of God is to be born from above. You are no longer operating under the bondage of earth's limitations but rather from above in the freedom of heaven's abundance. When you receive salvation you are officially victorious. You do not have to fight for victory but rather you can fight from your place of victory. You are designed by God and given a "Kingdom identity".

"But ye are a chosen generation, a royal priesthood, an holy nation, a peculiar people; that ye should shew forth the praises of him who hath called you out of darkness into his marvelous light"   1 Pet. 2:9

It matters not the shortcomings of your biological parents in the days of old. When God saved your soul through the shedding of His Son Jesus' blood you took on a new DNA. You are now a part of the royal family! This is why it is not wise to involve yourself in the cares of this life but rather to lay hold to the everlasting life that you inherit by the blood of Jesus. I know what many people will say, "Yes, I am royal, but I still have things that are in my life that contradict what the Word says." Your contradiction may be fact but according to the Gospel of John, the Word is designed to take care of those issues. John 8:32 states, "and ye shall know the truth, and the truth shall make you free". This is the revelation of God's will for His children - to live in victory and to know His truth. This empowers you to embrace trials and contradictions that attempt to hinder you. You now know that not only do you have the victory but also you can experience the omnipotent power of God in your life for yourself. Therefore, you build confidence and develop your faith during warfare. There will be times when you will seek improvement in areas of your life, whether it be in marriage, finances, ministry, health, etc., and what you see may not be what you want. But now nothing can stop you from extracting the promises of God from the unseen realm of Heaven and walking in your Kingdom inheritance in spite of Satan's attack of afflictions in the visible realm here on earth.

> *"While we look not at the things which are seen, but at the things which are not seen: for the things which are seen are temporal; but the things which are not seen are eternal"*
>
> 2 Cor. 4:18

You remember the cliché "what you see is what you get," but God has designed you in such a way that if what you see contradicts what He has said concerning your life, then you can speak those things that be not as though they were. The truth is the Word of God and it will manifest both freedom and deliverance in your life.

> *"Many are the afflictions of the righteous:*
> *but the LORD delivereth him out of them all"*
> *Psa. 34:19*

You are designed to be strengthened through your struggles. Oftentimes in life you can be like fish swimming up stream through the currents of the world's hatred all around you. But you must never develop hater claustrophobia. People are not successful because everyone applauds them. They are

---

GOD HAS DESIGNED YOU IN SUCH A WAY THAT IF WHAT YOU SEE CONTRADICTS WHAT HE HAS SAID CONCERNING YOUR LIFE, THEN YOU CAN SPEAK THOSE THINGS THAT BE NOT AS THOUGH THEY WERE.

---

not successful because they have a lot of support. They are successful because they stand up straight, square their shoulders, hold their head high and

VICTORIOUS LIVING

withstand the opposition and the criticism that is often associated with success. In fact many times success breeds contempt. People resent it. They are frustrated by it. They are angered by it and they are jealous of it. You have to understand that in order to keep your victory you cannot afford to expend your energy and your strength responding to your critics. Your critics can be proof positive signs that you are on the right track. They indicate to you that you are doing something right. People do not criticize people who are not doing anything. Mediocrity is never criticized. It is when you decide to grasp hold of victorious living and go beyond the norm that the criticisms come. It is when you stand out and you dare to be different. The uninformed voices from the peanut gallery cannot control you simply because they do not understand you. Let them misunderstand you. Those who do not honor you do not need to understand you! There is a natural tendency to want to be understood when you hear yourself misrepresented by others. You want to run to the person and say "that's not who I am" or "that's not what I meant".

You are designed to encourage yourself. You get a thing because you are determined to change your current situation; therefore, you say what you want to see and then you do what it takes to manifest it. Proverbs 18:21 says, "death and life are in the power of the tongue: and they that love it shall eat the fruit thereof". Encourage yourself with God's Word and love it and you will eat the fruit thereof because when you align your life with God's Word you are going to get what God's Word says you can have. It is a must, however, that you partner what you say with what you do.

> *"But be ye doers of the word, and not hearers only, deceiving your own selves" James 1:22*

You are designed to say it and do it. Although you may not be able to say it all or do it all in one day, you must make sure that you do not say or do a thing that will contradict your goal. Do not flip the script because Jeremiah 29:11 says, "for I know the thoughts that I think toward you, saith the LORD, thoughts of peace, and not of evil, to give you an expected end." God's plan for your life is everything you need, want, and

| VICTORIOUS LIVING

desire to have a life of blessings. In fact, He has the best plan. He has a predetermined life of peace and an expected end of prosperity for you. All that you have to do is lay hold of it. I call it a script, if you will. In life you are not an actor, however, you are called to play a role. This role has an interesting twist. You cannot simply walk off set and back into your normal life. In order to live victoriously you must live according to the will of God, and His will is the script that is written in His Holy Word.

> *"Looking unto Jesus the 'author and finisher of our faith'; who for the joy that was set before him endured the cross, despising the shame, and is set down at the right hand of the throne of God"*   Heb. 12:2

God is indeed the chief author. Your life is simply the manifestation of the plans that He has already written. According to Psalm 37:23 "the steps of a good man are ordered by the LORD: and he delighteth in his way". Many people wonder what they can do to maximize their lives. Oftentimes people make their lives too hard

PEOPLE ARE NOT SUCCESSFUL BECAUSE EVERYONE APPLAUDS THEM.

and take on undue burdens that God has reserved the right to handle Himself. That is why it states in 1 Peter 5:7 "casting all your care upon him; for he careth for you." To care for you simply means that He does not want you to worry about anything but rather have faith in His Word. His Word is the order that He has designed for you. In fact, victorious living is Heaven's will for your life.

> *"What is man, that thou art mindful of him? and the son of man, that thou visitest him? For thou hast made him a little lower than the angels, and hast crowned him with glory and honour. Thou madest him to have dominion over the works of thy hands; thou hast put all things under his feet"*   Psa. 8:4-6

As a believer you have a birth right of dominion over everything that God has created. What you have to do is spend time with God and learn how to hear His

| VICTORIOUS LIVING

voice clearly so that you can operate in the authority that He has given you. Jeremiah 33:3 says "call unto me, and I will answer thee, and shew thee great and mighty things, which thou knowest not". When you call upon the Lord He will begin to release unto you your Kingdom assignment.

MEDIOCRITY IS NEVER CRITICIZED.

You must be willing to let go of your confidence in man and place all of your faith in God. The script that is written is never the role you initially see yourself playing. You would naturally choose the leading role, however in the kingdom Jesus is the only star. You are a supporting cast member who takes the cue from the leading Man.

> *"THE LORD is my shepherd; I shall not want. He maketh me to lie down in green pastures: he leadeth me beside the still waters. He restoreth my soul: he leadeth me in the paths of righteousness for his name's sake"*
>
> *Psa. 23: 1 – 3*

As you continue to follow Christ, His will for your life will be continuously manifest. The purpose of Jesus Christ coming into the earth was to liberate those who were bound by the demonic forces of this world. But if there is a leader there must be a follower that receives instructions on how to stay out of the wilderness and how to stay in God's will. Never give your authority to the secular and deceiving entrapments in the earth because it is your inheritance to operate in authority over all of the works of the Father's hands. Your mind must be transformed into a Kingdom mindset of God in order to live in the authority and assurance of God. Many people make the vital mistake of relinquishing their God given authority in the earth because they conform to this world. God says we are placed over all the works of His hands so it makes no sense for us to bow to things that we are called to reign over. Time and time again we see someone who desires a house, car, or new employment and because of his or her impatience they have no peace in their heart. Many forfeit their Kingdom assignment to achieve their personal agenda and that is flipping the script. In fact, everyone has had an immature season that they have gone through in life. God instructs you on how to deal with this in the book of Hebrews.

> *"WHEREFORE seeing we also are compassed about with so great a cloud of witnesses, let us lay aside every weight, and the sin which doth so easily beset us, and let us run with patience the race that is set before us"*
>
> *Heb. 12:1*

When you lay aside every weight that means that you take all of your desires to God, and you become free from the "me factor". People who do not have their lives in proper alignment with God do not have confidence in their ability to walk in dominion as an heir of God. Your life purpose is in God's time and His will and when you are aware of this revelation you can find peace in adverse situations. Understanding who God is indicates you know who you are according to Genesis.

DESIGNED BY GOD | V

> *"So God created man in his own image, in the image of God created he him; male and female created he them"*   Gen. 1:27

Isaiah 9:6 tells us that God is an eternal and everlasting Father. With that in mind, understand that He is not confined to an earthly timetable but rather to His own timetable as an infinite God. As a child of God you must not be anxious when it comes to various seasons that you encounter in life. God knows your end and if He has not allowed some of His promises to manifest in your life yet it could only be either of two reasons:

1) ***You are not in His will.***
2) ***It is not time yet.***

Never fear that your expiration date is going to occur before your life's purpose is achieved. If you are living in His will you are right on schedule. Time does not work against those who are in the Father's will. True sons and daughters of God want to see progression in their lives. However, they must not get frazzled when it seems as if they are not getting what they

VICTORIOUS LIVING

need to advance into the next dimension. Thinking to themselves, "What about me? When is my blessing going to arrive? When am I going to be recognized for my loyalty to the organization and why is it that I am always overlooked and left out?" Let me remind you of the "David's Anointing".

> *"Now David was the son of that Ephrathite of Bethlehem-judah, whose name was Jesse; and he had eight sons: and the man went among men for an old man in the days of Saul. And the three eldest sons of Jesse went and followed Saul to the battle: and the names of his three sons that went to the battle were Eliab the firstborn, and next unto him Abinadab, and the third Shammah. And David was the youngest: and the three eldest followed Saul. But David went and returned from Saul to feed his father's sheep at Bethlehem"*
>
> 1 Sam. 1:12-15

While reading this passage I noticed that it said "but David went and returned from Saul to feed his father's sheep". Certainly he must have wanted to be a part of Saul's army. How honorable and just would such an opportunity have been to serve the regional king? But to whom? Why sure it would be an accolade among men, because man often notices and recognize us by our achievements. However in many instances we find ourselves majoring in achievements that yield recognition from man and minoring in events that causes recognition and approval from God. One thing that sticks out about David is his commitment to his "fathers" in every aspect of leadership. From Father God to Jesse to Samuel and on to King Saul, David was a man committed to his leadership and connected to the Lord. David knew that when Saul's army went to battle that he had an obligation to fulfill at home with his father Jesse. This obligation would cause him to forfeit his personal ambition to prosper and to ensure that the vision of his covering came to pass. When I look at David's other brothers, Eliab, Abinadab, and Shammah, I cannot even imagine that level of sacrifice going through their minds. David's brothers were opportunists, but when opportunity arrived and there had been no preparation, there was no anointing to

| VICTORIOUS LIVING

achieve the task at hand. We see this by the fact that when Goliath came against the children of God only David had the anointing to defeat him.

> *"For the gifts and calling of God are without repentance"*   Rom. 11:29

But the anointing comes from the Lord and the anointing is will based, meaning God does not have a vested interest in anointing anyone who rejects His will for their lives. The prerequisite for any degree of true leadership is found in Luke 16:12. It states "and if ye have not been faithful in that which is another man's, who shall give you that which is your own?". David knew how to trust God with his life. After all, if God is the giver of life certainly He knows what is best for you and the process in which He ordained you to prosper.

To live victoriously you must trust the process that God takes you through to fulfill your call. If you do not trust the process in which God designs to develop you for your destiny, you will never reach it. The sad part is that you will spend the rest of your life chasing success yet operating under the bondage of your own selfish ambitions rather than your ordained assignment.

WHAT YOU HAVE TO DO IS SPEND TIME WITH GOD AND LEARN HOW TO HEAR HIS VOICE CLEARLY SO THAT YOU CAN OPERATE IN THE AUTHORITY THAT HE HAS GIVEN YOU.

In the military we use the cliché "hurry up and wait". This speaks to the fact that often times the military is called to formation and given an exciting and tremendous assignment to accomplish. Yet, when asked "When shall we start?" the leadership replies "TBA" (to be announced), for right now that information is both critical and confidential. At first thought you think to yourself, "But wait a minute I need more Intel. What about me and about my life? How am I supposed to plan my life without more information? When am I going to get concrete information to base my future endeavors upon?" But what does the military say?

| VICTORIOUS LIVING

1) You are on twenty-four hour call.

2) Do not go beyond the distance allotted to your home base.

3) Be packed and ready to go at anytime.

4) Stay focused and continue operating in all of your normal tasking and duties.

YOUR LIFE PURPOSE IS IN GOD'S TIME AND HIS WILL AND WHEN YOU ARE AWARE OF THIS REVELATION YOU CAN FIND PEACE IN ADVERSE SITUATIONS.

In order to function in obedience in times such as these you must conclude that when God is doing a great work in your life He does not have to explain all of the details. In fact He refuses to because if God brought everything down to your human logic you would not be able to please Him. The Bible says in Hebrews 11:6 that without faith it is impossible to please the Lord. We cannot devalue our relationship with our Heavenly Father to a carnal acquaintance filled with human skepticism. Using the systematic formula of carnal friendship we hear what the other party has to say and leave each other's presence saying, "Yeah right, I'll believe it when I see it". No my friend, you will know it when you see it. The Bible tells us "for we are saved by hope: but hope that is seen is not hope: for what a man seeth, why doth he yet hope for?" (Rom. 8:24). It seems as if the only time we enjoy the element of surprise is when we are surprising someone else. In the Kingdom of God however, you are not in control of your own life. When you crown Him Lord you do so by saying, "Lord you are the head of my life." By doing so, you come under the submission and the will of your Heavenly Father in order to truly prosper and have the assurance of an abundant and everlasting life.

> *"Know ye that the LORD he is God: it is he that hath made us, and not we ourselves; we are his people, and the sheep of his pasture"*
>
> Psa. 100:3

> *"Thou art worthy, O Lord, to receive glory and honour and power: for thou hast created all things, and for thy pleasure they are and were created"*   Rev. 4:11

VICTORIOUS LIVING

The pleasure of the Lord is His love for His children made manifest in their lives. God takes pleasure in you when you obey Him because it causes His divine plan for your life to come to pass. There is no greater achievement to be accomplished than to fulfill the call of God on your life. A true son always seeks to please his father. Doing what is right will always yield the right results. After all, is it not that the heart of a good king to do what is right as unto the Lord and to serve and prefer others before himself? David was already operating as king and he never looked at it from the standpoint of losing an opportunity but rather gaining another chance to please the Father.

> *"His lord said unto him, Well done, thou good and faithful servant: thou hast been faithful over a few things, I will make thee ruler over many things: enter thou into the joy of thy lord"*   Matt. 25:21

God looks at our stewardship in the small areas of life. A steward is a person who manages another's property or financial affairs; one who administers anything as the agent of another or others. You own nothing in the earth outside of your partnership with God. Through the trials that Job overcame he received this revelation and penned Job 1:21 "and said, Naked came I out of my mother's womb, and naked shall I return thither".

> *"THE earth is the LORD's, and the fullness thereof; the world, and they that dwell therein"*   *Psa. 24:1*

It can become very easy to forget about the element of partnership and move into a position of total autonomy when it comes to your pursuits and goals. But when you come from under the Lordship of Christ you are no longer walking in victory but risk the chance of becoming a victim.

> *"Abide in me, and I in you. As the branch cannot bear fruit of itself, except it abide in the vine; no more can ye, except ye abide in me."*   *John 15:4*

| VICTORIOUS LIVING

Time does not work against those who are in the Father's will.

Here are keys of the David's Anointing that will cause Victorious Living:

1. *Anointed to Focus*

David was a man with incredible focus. Though he was no doubt far more devoted and honorable than his brothers, he never let the lack of appreciation from others derail his dedication to the work of the Lord. What others considered to be a menial task, David considered important. David pursued and achieved all of his ministry assignments with excellence and dedication. When pursuing your destiny always remember that when you become frustrated by lack of affirmation from man that your faith should always be in God. When your faith is in any other person, place or thing, it is misplaced. Your faith is in He who has called you and He alone shall cause you to prosper. Never depend on man to do the right thing. John 15:18 says, "if the world hate you, ye know that it hated me before it hated you". There are fiery darts of the enemy such as racism, where people refuse to promote you because of the color of your skin, or jealousy where people speak negatively about you to others because there is nothing positive going on in their lives. Nonetheless, God will cause you to reign in victory if you continue to stay the course. Remember Romans 8:28 states, "and we know that all things work together for good to them that love God, to them who are the called according to his purpose."

TO LIVE VICTORIOUSLY YOU MUST TRUST THE PROCESS THAT GOD TAKES YOU THROUGH TO FULFILL YOUR CALL.

---

2. *Anointed with Humility*
Certainly every son desires affirmation from his father; however David took no offense to his father's lack of consideration for his future endeavors. We often position ourselves for promotion by bettering ourselves through different classes or acquiring training certificates. David's job was not one that was easily cross-trainable. For sure, once you are the sheep boy you are pretty much stuck and find that there are very few mentors and even fewer mentees that can see

| VICTORIOUS LIVING

the value of humble beginnings. But David knew that one day in the presence of the Lord was much more than 1,000 days in the presence of man. He knew that his spiritual positioning with the will of God had to be aligned in order for his physical promotion to manifest.

> *"But he that is greatest among you shall be your servant. And whosoever shall exalt himself shall be abased; and he that shall humble himself shall be exalted"*
>
> Matt. 23:11-12

Humility is the gateway to promotion. When someone is humble they are certain of their inheritance from God. They never suffer anxiety from the lack of equality, respect, and fairness in this world because they understand that God will always supply what the earth neglects to yield. God brings comfort to you through His word concerning this in Philippians 4:19 when Paul says, "but my God shall supply all your need according to his riches in glory by Christ Jesus". When you know this it aids your endurance in the heat of battle. You often hear about the strength of David;

however, what you have to ask yourself is "Was David ever frustrated by some of the things that occurred in his life while he awaited his breakthrough?" Why, sure he was! Anyone doing anything that is worth something has moments of dissatisfaction during the process toward his or her success. Of course we have to stand strong in front of others, but we all have had secret conversations between man and flesh. These conversations are orchestrated with one vision in mind and that is to try to convince you to quit. Yes! Every good Apostle, Prophet, Evangelist, Teacher, Pastor, Minister, Deacon, Armor bearer, Usher, and every other form of Kingdom leadership has had these conversations. It can be a sigh of relief to know that you are not the only one who encounters these emotions. However, you must be aware that the very act of this conversation is not humility but rather it is the flesh and pride beginning to rise up, stand up, and exalt itself. How did David stay humble even through the entrapments of his own flesh? It was not his love for being a shepherd boy, but it was his love for the Shepherd of his soul. You can stay humble if you stay in God because God is love.

| VICTORIOUS LIVING

> *"And we have known and believed the love that God hath to us. God is love; and he that dwelleth in love dwelleth in God, and God in him"*   1 John 4:16

So we have to stay in love in order to operate in victory. You cannot use hate because haters cannot walk in divine authority because they are not in God. They have been either pulled out or refuse to step in.

Dr. Martin Luther King Jr. showed us how to walk in love. In my opinion, there has been no greater display of humility publicly in this era than Dr. King because his stand was a Kingdom sacrifice that made a global difference. Many of his own African American brothers became frustrated with him because they did not understand God's order. They desired to use hatred instead of love, but Dr. King stilled the people and he would not let hate reign. Dr. King knew that only the love of God could cause freedom for his people and love is the only thing that can defeat hate. We see the attributes of love in the following scriptures:

"Hatred stirreth up strifes: but love covereth all sins"   *Pro. 10:12*

"Charity suffereth long, and is kind; charity envieth not; charity vaunteth not itself, is not puffed up"   *1 Cor.13: 4*

"And we have known and believed the love that God hath to us. God is love; and he that dwelleth in love dwelleth in God, and God in him"   *1 John 4:16*

The love that God has for you is beyond comprehension, strategy, and calculation. And when you stay in love it gives you access to everything that Heaven has for you. The god of this world knows about your access and understands that his time is running out. Therefore, as you wait on your heavenly release Satan tries to distract you and cause discomfort in your daily life. His efforts are to try to pull you out of your Heavenly Father's love with hopes that you will abandon God's will for your life. Can't you just hear Satan's demonic chatter that David had to endure while tending to his fathers

| VICTORIOUS LIVING

sheep? David had to press his way through the seeds of doubt such as: "Life is just passing you by. You are out here in this field while everyone else is relaxing. Why don't they ever ask others to assist you while you work out here. You should tell your leadership that if they don't hurry up and get you some help that you are going to have to resign from this ministry. Out of everyone that they could have asked to do this job, why did they ask you to do this one? Is this all that they think of you? Do you see how insignificant you are to your family, your job, and to your ministry?" This kind of satanic attack can easily break a weak individual down. But David was far from a weak man. So often people mistake meekness for weakness but David was humble and confident that God would make a way. When humble before the Lord your humility becomes a target for God's blessing. The Word of the

---

HOWEVER, NEVER COMPLAIN ABOUT WHERE YOU ARE BECAUSE THAT SAYS TO GOD, YOU DO NOT APPRECIATE WHAT HE HAS DONE FOR YOU.

Lord declares "abide in me, and I in you. As the branch cannot bear fruit of itself, except it abide in the vine; no more can ye, except ye abide in me" (John 15:4). When the light of God is in you, it is in the midst of the darkness of this world that your assignment is revealed. Never subjugate your Kingdom assignment to earthly limitations. By doing so you become co-dependent on the god of this world. But when you understand that, as an heir of God, you have ownership of the earth and Satan is merely a tenant that is getting evicted daily, you are not worried about how it looks on the outside. It may seem as if injustice is being done but you know what the Word says according to 1 John 4:4, "ye are of God, little children, and have overcome them: because greater is he that is in you, than he that is in the world". Furthermore, Philippians 4:19 says, "but my God shall supply all your need according to his riches in glory by Christ Jesus".

A Heart that Trusts God

David learned how to trust God. He never gave God a carnal ultimatum or time line to promote him. Can't you just hear someone saying "Lord I'm going to give

| VICTORIOUS LIVING

this sheep herding about a year or two at best and if I don't see anything prospering me you are going to have to find me another field, i.e., ministry"? But David never allowed his ambitions to interfere with God's assignment for his life. No wonder he was able to pen the following Psalm:

> *"Trust in the LORD, and do good; so shalt thou dwell in the land, and verily thou shalt be fed. Delight thyself also in the LORD; and he shall give thee the desires of thine heart"*
>
> *Psa. 37: 3 – 4*

He is a living witness that when you stay the course and endure, you are not forfeiting any blessings but rather compelling God to bless you. Zechariah 4:10 states "for who hath despised the day of small things?". Do not look at where you are and think that the Lord has abandoned you. Where you are is not where you are going. However, never complain about where you are because that says to God, you do not appreciate what He has done for you. Remember Jesus was born in a manger. The earthly accommodations of His birth were far from the Ritz Carlton experience, however the Savior manages to make do. Your humble beginnings are used to work miraculous endings that are a witness for the whole world to see God's glory upon your life.

> *"The glory of this latter house shall be greater than of the former, saith the LORD of hosts: and in this place will I give peace, saith the LORD of hosts"*   Hag. 2:9

VICTORIOUS LIVING

CHAPTER VI

DAVID'S ANOINTING

A Warrior's Anointing

"And David said unto Saul, Thy servant kept his father's sheep, and there came a lion, and a bear, and took a lamb out of the flock: And I went out after him, and smote him, and delivered it out of his mouth: and when he arose against me, I caught him by his beard, and smote him, and slew him. Thy servant slew both the lion and the bear: and this uncircumcised Philistine shall be as one of them, seeing he hath defied the armies of the living God. David said moreover, The LORD that delivered me out of the paw of the lion, and out of the paw of the bear, he will deliver

VICTORIOUS LIVING

> *me out of the hand of this Philistine. And Saul said unto David, Go, and the LORD be with you"*   1 Sam. 17:34 – 37

David developed the spirit of a warrior as a servant. It is being faithful in the unseen that we are taught to overcome. Others do not see the struggles or the times of hardship. Nonetheless, these elements of your life cultivate endurance and courage to overcome and to achieve victory over future obstacles in greater realms. David approached today's problems as tomorrow's praise reports and faced all of them with a prophetic word of victory even before the fight began.

ABLE TO RECEIVE THE PROMISE AND FULFILL THE CALL

> *"Then Samuel took the horn of oil, and anointed him in the midst of his brethren: and the Spirit of the LORD came upon David from that day forward. So Samuel rose up, and went to Ramah"*   1 Sam. 16:13

DAVID'S ANOINTING | VI

> **DAVID KNEW THAT NO MATTER HOW THINGS FLUCTUATED IN THE EARTH REALM HE HAD A HEAVENLY PROMISE, AND TO SEE IT MANIFEST ALL HE HAD TO DO WAS PLEASE GOD.**

Here we see the Prophet Samuel anointing David and speaking into him what Heaven had declared. What is most impressive is that David could receive a heavenly Word, which is the promise that was yet to come, and still not abandon the call, which is his earthly responsibilities. Can you discern the humility of such a man? He was anointed by God's set man yet he never abandoned the divine order of God with full knowledge that he had to return and submit to the king he was chosen to replace, with no projected date of upward mobility. David knew that no matter how things fluctuated in the earth realm he had a heavenly promise, and to see it manifest all he had to do was please God. Afterall, it was Saul's displeasure to God that made the promotion possible in the first place.

VICTORIOUS LIVING

Kingdom Paradigm

Notice that David was anointed by Samuel and received the prophecy of his throne in the 16th chapter of 1 Samuel, yet in the 17th chapter we see that the fulfillment of the prophecy was far from its manifestation. We find David not only speaking to the fact that he had to fight a bear and a lion, also being faced with the task of defeating a giant. Having a Kingdom paradigm does not mean that you will not have giants to defeat. In fact, the giants that you face on your way to the top are proof positive that you are indeed chosen by God. With this revelation, your mind is not in fear of the giant but confident of your victory. David had the heart of the father, which gave him the spirit of a finisher. When you are chosen to accomplish a Kingdom assignment, the initial calling can be very encouraging but there are experiences that you have to go through that seem to contradict the vision. When you obey you can sometimes think that you are excluded from hardship and drama, but you must not allow these occurrences to become a false detour sign and turn around prematurely before you reach your goal.

DAVID'S ANOINTING | VI

"And Jesus said unto him, No man, having put his hand to the plough, and looking back, is fit for the kingdom of God"   Luke 9:62

Many people in leadership have the ability to quote the scriptures and name it and claim it. That is what you are supposed to do; however it is much easier to talk about it than to do it. David was a doer who exercised faith in action by completing his God given assignment.

"And it came to pass, when the Philistine arose, and came and drew nigh to meet David, that David hasted, and ran toward the army to meet the Philistine. And David put his hand in his bag, and took thence a stone, and slang it, and smote the Philistine in his forehead, that the stone sunk into his forehead; and he fell upon his face to the earth. So David prevailed over the Philistine with a sling and with a stone, and smote the Philistine, and slew him; but there was no sword in the hand of David. Therefore David

| VICTORIOUS LIVING

> *ran, and stood upon the Philistine, and took his sword, and drew it out of the sheath thereof, and slew him, and cut off his head therewith. And when the Philistines saw their champion was dead" 1 Sam. 17:48 – 51*

The heart of God was released to David in the instructions that he received from God. Notice he did not hesitate once he received a word from the Lord. In verse 48 the Word declares that David ran towards his enemy because he had a word from the Lord, and in David's mind, if God said it that settled it.

DAVID HAD AN ANOINTING TO REIGN

> *"And the men of Judah came, and there they anointed David king over the house of Judah. And they told David, saying, That the men of Jabesh-gilead were they that buried Saul"*
>
> *2 Sam. 2:4*

After enduring all of the years of hardship, trials, agony, and pain, David received the manifestation of the prophetic word of Samuel from when he had anointed

DAVID'S ANOINTING | VI

him many years prior as the King of Israel. When you look at the nuances of this miraculous story you must admit that the prior sequence of events are certainly not the experiential qualifications that one endures to become a general, prime minister, or president. These are all positions that are given by man. But when there is a heavenly calling there is only one Man who reserves the right to announce promotion.

> *"For promotion cometh neither from the east, nor from the west, nor from the south. But God is the judge: he putteth down one, and setteth up another"* Psa. 75: 6-7

Therefore, be encouraged in your walk with Christ and stay the course. One question that I am often asked is "How do you know that you are in God's will?". The will of God is released through the voice of the Holy Spirit and when you are obedient to the Holy Spirit you are in His will.

| VICTORIOUS LIVING

> *"But the Comforter, which is the Holy Ghost, whom the Father will send in my name, he shall teach you all things, and bring all things to your remembrance, whatsoever I have said unto you"*   John 14:26

The Holy Ghost will teach you the will of God for your life. You do not have to guess whether or not you are in the will of God, just continue on His plan and trust Him to lead you into victory. David always prayed to God and every time he got an answer. The key to his success is that he always implemented what God said.

LOYALTY

David was very loyal and his love for God was unchanging. When faced with crisis, carnal Christians draw back from their pursuit of righteousness, but David drew closer to the Lord in the time of trouble. He knew that a crisis was not the time to lose faith in God but it was the time to learn more about the God in whom he put his faith. The sign of your maturity is shown in your ability to trust God's plan for your life when things are going wrong. Even when things seem to be going down hill you must continue to walk upright.

> *"For the LORD God is a sun and shield: the LORD will give grace and glory: no good thing will he withhold from them that walk uprightly"*
>
> Psa. 84:11

> *"But without faith it is impossible to please him: for he that cometh to God must believe that he is, and that he is a rewarder of them that diligently seek him"* Heb. 11:6

David had faith under fire and his pursuit of God and trust in His word surely paid off. When you are faithful to God and embrace the plans that he has for your life, you to can find yourself overcoming the hard times of this life and entering into the destiny of the Kingdom. One of life's greatest challenge is locating your Kingdom assignment. The only way that you can truly do this is to exercise the gifts of the Holy Spirit.

| VICTORIOUS LIVING

KINGDOM ASSIGNMENT

The Holy Spirit is the intimate means of communication between God and man that releases the intent, will, nature, morals, values, and desires of God in your life, as well as the lives of those directly connected to your Kingdom assignment. The Holy Spirit also guides you in your Kingdom assignment:

1. *To be saved*
To be saved is to be free from the eternal damnation that this world brings. It means receiving immunity from the plans of Satan for your life by becoming a citizen of the Kingdom.

| **VICTORIOUS** LIVING

2. ***To be an overcomer***

> "For whatsoever is born of God overcometh the world: and this is the victory that overcometh the world, even our faith"
>
> 1 John 5:4

To overcome the bondage of this world by enduring the contradictions and suffering that they bring. The only way to establish the victory of the Kingdom in the earth is to overcome the tests and trials that you face from day to day.

3. ***To be a witness***

> "And they overcame him by the blood of the Lamb, and by the word of their testimony; and they loved not their lives unto the death"
>
> Rev. 1:11

> "Go ye therefore, and teach all nations, baptizing them in the name of the Father, and of the Son, and of the Holy Ghost"
>
> Matt. 28:19

KINGDOM ASSIGNMENT | VII

Once you overcome there is a Kingdom obligation to free others with your testimony.

Victorious living understands the heart of God. The heart of God towards His children is to see them live in righteousness and royalty. Both of these attributes are a part of your Kingdom identity. You see this when Jesus says in John 10:10 "the thief cometh not, but for to steal, and to kill, and to destroy: I am come that they might have life, and that they might have it more abundantly." The thief is Satan and when he was cast out of Heaven he purposed in his heart to torment every human being in the earth so that they would not have the relationship with the Heavenly Father that he lost.

> *"How art thou fallen from heaven, O Lucifer, son of the morning! how art thou cut down to the ground, which didst weaken the nations! For thou hast said in thine heart, I will ascend into heaven, I will exalt my throne above the stars of God: I will sit also upon the mount of the congregation, in the sides of the north"*
>
> Isa. 14:12 – 13

VICTORIOUS LIVING

Notice after God cast Satan down how Satan spoke of sitting upon the mount of the congregation. This means that he desires to head the congregation or control their minds. He lost his Kingdom identity and everyday he launches an attack to try to keep you from yours. He deceives people so that they will not receive the blessings of God causing them to become too afraid to believe that the unseen God has power over their seen situations. But God wants us to know that Satan is a defeated foe. Although you may have been uncertain of your Kingdom identity in past times Jesus says that I have come to give you life. Before you accept Jesus Christ into your life you lack identity, and this is why the Word of God in Romans 12 calls it conformity or

> **BUT GOD WANTS US TO KNOW THAT SATAN IS A DEFEATED FOE.**

taking on the likeness of the world. The life that Jesus came to give you is citizenship in God's Kingdom. This life is about living in prosperity. Jesus says to you that He has come that you might have life more abundantly. Whatever the enemy does to hurt you, God is always doing more to help you. Therefore, no matter what the enemy tries to do, you are abundantly equipped with power, wealth and protection from God to overcome any and everything and you will continue to prosper.

Prosperity

Prosperity is the Kingdom way of thinking, living, and having a life that is thriving and flourishing. The only way to really receive your Kingdom inheritance is through mind renewal. When you are not in the mind of God you are not in the will of God. The will of God entails all of the purposes and plans that God has for your life.

> *"For I know the thoughts that I think toward you, saith the LORD, thoughts of peace, and not of evil, to give you an expected end"*
>
> Jer. 29:11

God knows what you do not know. You must understand that He releases 'intel' to you on a need to know basis. What is most vital when facing hardships and trials is that you know God still has a purpose and

| VICTORIOUS LIVING

a plan in all that you go through. It is all about what you know. "Know" is the root word for "knowledge" and this is what Paul prayed for as it pertains to the saints.

> *"For this cause we also, since the day we heard it, do not cease to pray for you, and to desire that ye might be filled with the knowledge of his will in all wisdom and spiritual understanding; That ye might walk worthy of the Lord unto all pleasing, being fruitful in every good work, and increasing in the knowledge of God"*   Col. 1: 9-10

Why did Paul pray this prayer? Paul knew that if the church would limit its relationship with God to just the death, the burial, and the resurrection that, yes, we would be saved and able to return with Jesus when He comes, but we would not reign in victory in the interim of time while we awaited Him. So the Bible says in John 14:16 "and I will pray the Father, and he shall give you another Comforter, that he may abide with you for ever". Why does the Comforter need to do this? The Comforter is the mind of God and without the mind of God within you Satan will come into your natural mind and sow seeds of fear, doubt, and unbelief. Battles are won and lost in your mind.

> *"And be not conformed to this world: but be ye transformed by the renewing of your mind, that ye may prove what is that good, and acceptable, and perfect, will of God"*
> *Rom. 12:2*

When your mind is renewed you become aligned with the perfect will of God. The perfect will of God is that you live according to 1 Peter 2:9 which states, "but ye are a chosen generation, a royal priesthood, an holy nation, a peculiar people; that ye should shew forth the praises of him who hath called you out of darkness into his marvelous light". This scripture tells you who you are. You can never look to the world to confirm who you are, but you must understand that everything you need to fulfill God's plan for your life is inside of

VICTORIOUS LIVING

you. John 7:38 says, "he that believeth on me, as the scripture hath said, out of his belly shall flow rivers of living water".

Victory lies within every believer. Just as the metamorphosis of the butterfly from an egg, to a caterpillar, to a cocoon, to a butterfly. God predetermines every cycle of life. If you allow the Holy Spirit to lead you on your course, what God places in you will come out of you. Remember, this in your life today. Although there may be several seasons of change inside of you, God has already given you victorious living.

Notes

Chapter 4

The Pursuit of Happyness. By Steve Conrad. Dir. Gabriele Muccino. Perf. Will Smith, Thandie Newton and Jaden Smith 2006. Columbia Pictures.

| **VICTORIOUS** LIVING

About the Author

Dr. C.L. Spells, Sr. is the senior pastor and co-founder, with his wife Christina, of Harvest Land Ministries International Hampton, Virginia. A progressive ministry whose commitment and dedication to the great commission of the gospel has increased the quality of life of their followers, and caused souls to be saved across the region. Dr. Spells is an Apostolic and Prophetic preacher and teacher of the gospel. His exciting delivery and passion for God has created a powerful impact of miracles, signs and wonders in the lives of believers. Dr. Spells is the Regional Overseer of Living Waters International Alliance.

Dr. Spells is a forerunner and a faith instructor who teaches Kingdom principles and cutting edge concepts with an unwavering conviction to ever increase the faith of believers across the world. This dynamic Kingdom servant is also the author of *The Faith Realm: Increase in Spiritual Rank and Authority*. In this book, he masterfully explores the perilous issues that work against the successful operation of faith. The Faith Realm strips away the common errors and misconceptions surrounding faith to reveal the nature, character, and power of faith. The principles of faith are God's design to bring you everything you need. He is a man of global vision and destiny. This preacher, teacher, and life-coach is changing the lives of people across the nation, motivating them to believe God for the impossible. He has the vision to raise up a remnant of people to speak to trials and tribulations with power and authority.

www.ingramcontent.com/pod-product-compliance
Lightning Source LLC
Chambersburg PA
CBHW071146090426
42736CB00012B/2251